GOLF
The Agony & The Ecstasy

Eric Nicol & Dave More

GOLF

The Agony & The Ecstasy

Hurtig Publishers
Edmonton

Hurtig Publishers Ltd.
10560–105 Street
Edmonton, Alberta

Canadian Cataloguing in Publication Data

Nicol, Eric, 1919–
  Golf, the agony & the ecstasy

  ISBN 0-88830-218-5

  1. Golf—Anecdotes, facetiae, satire, etc.
2. Canadian wit and humor (English).*
I. More, Dave. II. Title.
GV967.N52   796.352'02'07   C82-091197-6

Printed and bound in Canada
by T.H. Best Company Limited

Contents

Fore!word/7

Ancient Gouffe (?–1774 A.D.)/11

Modern Golf (1774 A.D.–?)/23

This Vale of Tees/43

Vestments & Paraphernalia/79

Rites & Mysteries/107

Scoring & Other Myths/133

Is Golf for Eternity?/149

Sacro-mental Quiz/159

Sunday devotions
(or: Taking communion)

Fore!word

olf is a religion. No one questions that fact. The proof: People play Golf on Sunday, except doctors, for whom the sabbath falls on Thursday.

Golfers perform their arcane rites in a communal silence that makes the Trappist monks sound like "Let's Make a Deal." When Golfers do utter a word, in their votary rounds, it is the Lord's name—"O Jesus!", "Godalmighty!", "Gadzooks!" (originally "God's hooks," meaning divinely inspired flights of the ball that deviate from a straight course, in a direction opposite to the dominant hand of the player propelling it).

People who lose faith in Golf commonly convert to Catholicism, because the rules are easier to live with. Others take heavily to drink, or bowling, or both, and, like Falstaff, die babbling of green fields.

So much for the obvious. One question remains unanswered—or was until the authors of this book dared to address themselves to the forbidden subject: *Is Golf a dangerous sect?*

One elderly Golfer was asked: "Do you believe in the Golf cult?" He replied: "No, I carry my bag."

This man was partly deaf. Why? Was his hearing impaired by a lifetime of mortifying the flesh, keeping his head rigid while the rest of his body tried to screw

itself into the ground? Simulation tests with mice have been inconclusive. It is not difficult to teach mice to play Golf—they hit a bead-sized ball with their tails—if rewarded with a sip of Scotch. Ninety per cent of the test mice go mad, however, before the effect of Golf on their health can be accurately measured.

This statistic does, however, provide a clue for a study into the more subtle damage done by Golf to its divotees. (The term *divotee* was coined by followers of the nineteenth-century English Golfer Putney Flubb, who with a single swing extracted an enormous divot, took a stroke, fell into the grave and was covered by the descending sod, all without disturbing the ball.) How do we draw the line between freedom of religion and the right of the Golf pro to attract followers whose spiritual submission has been compared to that of the "moonies," the religious sect that indoctrinates the susceptible without charging green fees?

Distraught parents have sought to have their Golfing child de-programmed before they reached the critical point of paying for Golf clubs. Having forcibly rescued their son or daughter from the course, they hire a specialist to attempt the long and difficult task of convincing the brainwashed youngster that Heaven is not reserved for people who break a hundred. More often than not it is the de-programmer who backslides into a gully, up to his hips in thistle. Golf has that kind of power over the mind, after the age of eighteen months.

Here the authors (since exorcised) draw on their

personal experience as Golfers. One of them, who has asked not to be identified, was so possessed by Golf as a teenager that all his most ecstatic dreams revolved around finding Golf balls. The succubus that seduced him wore Argyle socks. At an age when other, normal young men were having nocturnal phantasies about the ideal girl, the author was waking up wet with excitement after a dream in which he lifted a fig leaf and found a brand new Titleist.

Against this cultist possession we must balance the possibility that if a person were not a Golfer he might succumb to some even more masochistic order, such as the flagellants, or jogging.

Do we judge Golf to be a benign form of Christianity, or a demoniac order whose victims are held in thrall by forces only dimly understood, even by the bar steward? The authors do not presume to know. All they can attempt is to capture something of the agony and the ecstasy that characterize the strange enchantment that is Golf. This present volume is devoted mainly to the agony. The ecstasy will be treated later, as a pamphlet.

EN & DM

Ancient Gouffe
(?–1774 A.D.)

Genesis of the family membership

priest, playing
Golf, missed the ball several times. He resorted to
prayer. Again he missed. Once more he prayed.
Again, a whiff. At last his caddy said: "Father, when
you pray—keep your head down."

(Old Golf joke)

Many a true word is spoken in jest. The Golfer at his
devotions assumes the classic attitude of prayer: head
bowed, hands clasped before the body, knees slightly
bent to absorb the impact of God's will. Except for the
shaft around which his fingers are clenched, he could

be celebrating communion in almost any church of the western world. The Golfer also conforms to the eastern world by adopting one of the other two attitudes of worship—genuflexion, and prostration (see page 83).

It is easy to see why the orthodox church feels threatened by Golf. The Pope does not play Golf. Those pastors who do sneak out on the links, on weekdays, justify their apostasy by saying that they are trying to learn what is the occult power of Golf that lures their parishioners from the pews on Sunday.

In this they fail. Although the Reverend Jones subjects himself to 18, 36, even 54 holes in quest to understand the passion with which he is talking to himself, he lacks scriptural reference. Until now.

Pilgrim's Progress

Now it can be stated with authority that Golf, as a weird religion, dates from the misty vales of prehistory. The word itself (Golf) derives from the Scandinavian word *gouffe*, or club. Some confusion has existed here, because in Golf the word *club* has two different meanings: (1) the group of members, usually found in the bar, and (2) the knobby instrument used to propel the ball, fell trees, and serve as a splint.

It now seems apparent, however, that the original gouffe was the club without the secretary-treasurer. Does this mean that Golf was created by the Vikings? Not at all. Golf appeared early in Ancient Britain, the game crossing the North Sea several times, probably because the wind caught a bad slice. On the evidence, the Vikings had sets of clubs (gouffes), but the ball came later. What they brought to Golf was the fierce language that distinguished the wielder of the club ("a Norse of a different choler," as one historian noted, just before he died).

Anthropologists such as Raymond Dart have established that the first club used by the ape-man to sap baboons was the upper foreleg of the common antelope. "Its heavy double-knobbed knuckle," says Robert Ardrey, in *African Genesis*, "fitted perfectly the double depression in the baboon skulls." Is it possible that one particularly vigorous ape-man swung his club with such force that he decapitated the baboon, the head rolling into a fox burrow to become the first hole-in-one? It is a beguiling thought.

Did man start walking upright because of Golf?

Golf martyr (Roman era)

Most evolutionists agree that man became erect in order to see over tall grass. Other species, that stayed out of the rough, had no incentive to stand on their hind legs unless they joined a circus. On all fours, the bag slung over their shoulder, their clubs kept falling out. They therefore failed to evolve, as man has evolved, into a creature capable of walking as a biped for distances up to seven thousand yards, before subsiding into the simian posture in the locker-room.

Whatever the genesis of the anatomy of Golf, its elevation to a religion dates from the time of the Druids. Indeed, Golf may in fact have begun as a splinter group to whom were sacred the bull and the bough. Golfers perhaps started as a Druidic sect that worshipped the sun but carried an umbrella just in case.

This introduces us to the authors' hypothesis that it was not the Druids who built Stonehenge but the Golfers. The so-called mystery of the great monoliths set out in the plains of Wiltshire dissipates like morning fog when we see that *Stonehenge was the first country Golf club*.

Examine pages 18 through 20. At once it becomes clear why this structure was placed in the middle of gently rolling country, miles from the nearest town: the Golfers, at that time an entirely male cult, wanted a clubhouse remote enough from their womenfolk to be able to practise their rituals, yet not so deep into the wilderness as to become prey to other wild animals.

The theory that the stones were arranged so as to

The Strange Rites of Stonehenge: (1) Putting in fear of sunset

The Strange Rites of Stonehenge: (2) Members' Lounge

permit astrological observations, to be in line with the
rising and setting sun at the equinox and so on, is
rubbish. The lines of sight were exquisitely calculated
so that the Golfers could see their wives coming in
good time. Similarly, the horseshoe design of the
double rows of gigantic slabs indicates that the early
Golfers believed in the influence of Luck. We can
picture each foursome reverently kissing the stones of
the horseshoe before mounting the first tee (later
called The Slaughter Stone).

Here we must consider briefly the controversial question: Did primitive Golf involve human sacrifice? Even today it is impossible to stand in the ruins of Stonehenge without seeming to hear tortured screams echoing down the dog's-leg of Time. It is more than likely that in the pre-Christian era Golfers sought to propitiate the Golf god by stoning the oldest member to death with round, white pebbles. On the other hand, the awesome dimensions of the stones may have invited no violence beyond a sturdy wall for the Golfers to bang their heads against, after a particularly grim round.

Less arguable is that the thirty-two "holes" of Stonehenge constituted the club's putting green. The holes are larger than today's because it was not till later that religious persecution of Golfers made it necessary to adopt a ball small enough to be hidden in the mouth without distending the cheeks. Thus began the modern era of Golf.

Modern Golf (1774 A.D.–?)

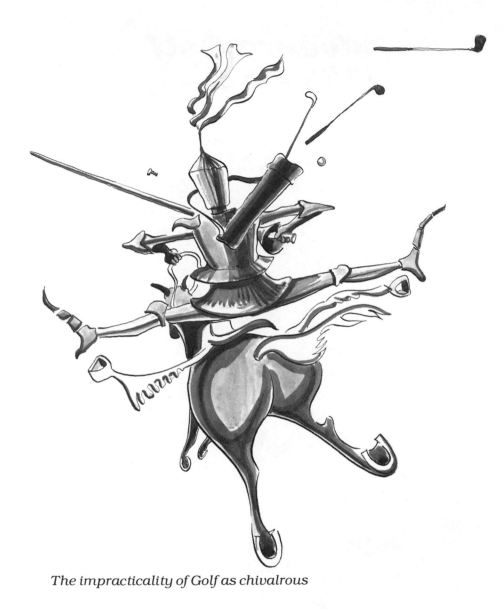

The impracticality of Golf as chivalrous

ccording to one elementary school of Golf historians, Golfing knights took part in the Crusades. This is absurd. To assume that the Crusades represented the first pro Golf tour, simply because the Syrian desert offered the challenge of the world's most hallowed sandtrap, ignores the facts. For one thing, the Crusaders were mounted. There is some evidence that early Scots may indeed have tried clubbing the ball while sitting on a Shetland pony. Some have theorized that Golf developed from this as a form of polo for people who could not afford to buy a horse. This is, however, elitist. Mounted golf, if it

Origin of the hammer throw

ever existed, died with the ground rule that unplayable balls must be dropped over the shoulder. Today only sheep and deer are allowed on the Golf course, in the Golfer's quest for a round object to smite.

As everyone knows, modern Golf had its beginning in Scotland, as an alternative to invading England. Some time during the Middle Ages, the first rounds were played on the grass-tufted, sandy downs of the eastern seaboard of Scotland (the "missing links"). Where exactly was the first Scottish Golf course? The clues point to a stretch of lifeless dunes north of Aberdeen. It is the only beach in the world

that is improved by an oil spill. Biological tests indicate that all forms of vegetation perished along the fore-shore during the thirteenth century, apparently as the result of repeated abuse of the soil to a depth of several feet. Even today any seed planted in this area grows downward instead of up, as if terrified of what it may encounter above ground. Also, primitive Golf clubs have been found on the sea bottom as far as a mile from shore, silent witness to the force with which the early Scottish Golfer hurled himself into the exaspera-tion that is such a vital part of the game.

Were the bagpipes invented when a Golfer became

27

so distraught with his stricken bag of clubs that he tried to give it mouth to mouth resuscitation? The point is moot. Less in dispute is the fact that the more warlike clans did carry their Golf clubs into battle, striking terror into the foe faced with the particularly prolonged agony of this gelding weapon.

Because Golf could be adapted to bloodshed even better than other Christian faiths, by the fifteenth century it had become so popular that Scotland often forgot why it had gone to war. Thus King James IV (Acts, 1491) decreed: "That in na place in the realme thair be usit fut-ballis, golf or other sic unprofitabill sportis."

From the spelling of this injunction it is plain that the Scottish monarch had tried Golf and it destroyed his mind. His use of the word "unprofitabill" (just one year before Christopher Columbus in 1492 sailed across the ocean blue to discover the riches of the New World) is symptomatic of the manic depression of a sovereign who has lost so many Golf balls that he has become unhinged. James IV bogeyed the last years of his reign by making an alliance with the French, who did not play Golf but were Catholic. Against the advice of his counsellors he marched against England and was killed at the battle of Flodden (1512), most of the Scottish aristocracy being annihilated before they could draw their niblick.

Such religious persecution made the Golfers of Scotland realize that Golf needed a basilica of the stature of Notre Dame de Paris, or the Great Mosque of

Scottish Independence

Lahore. Thus they founded in 1774 The Royal and Ancient Golf Club of St. Andrews.

It would be difficult to place too much significance on the fact that Golf's holy of holies was named after the patron saint of Scotland. The Bible does not say a great deal about Andrew. He seems to have popped up when the apostles needed a fourth. However, tradition casts him as a missionary in Asia Minor, meaning that he walked great distances without regard for personal suffering. Inevitably, his name is sacred to Golfers.

It should also be noted that The Royal and Ancient Golf Club of St. Andrews is two years older than the American Revolution. It also antedates the French Revolution. This may explain why there was no Scottish Revolution: life, liberty and the pursuit of happiness were frivolous goals to people trying to reach the first green in two.

The severity of Golf orthodoxy according to St. Andrews is well known. No Golfer steps on that immutable turf without remembering that here, within living memory, a caddy was publicly executed for allowing the flag to touch the ground. Golfers from all over the world make the pilgrimage to St. Andrews and—the opposite of Lourdes—leave broken in mind and body. Golfers who have known nothing but the easy virtues of snap courses, in sunny havens such as Bermuda and Las Vegas, return home from the religious experience of St. Andrews so prostrated that friends and family have to help them remove the twigs of heather stuffed up their nose.

Other Golf courses may be more cruelly laid out, but none is better designed to combine the Spanish Inquisition with outdoor living.

In January, 1981, the hallowed halls were shaken by the news that the government had granted an oil company a licence to explore the links. For Golfdom, this was the equivalent of granting drilling rights in the Vatican. The depth of the hole permitted on St. Andrews has been ordained for centuries: four inches. Any oil rig that probes deeper will be automatically excommunicated as an instrument of the Devil.

"Blasphemous" was the word used by St. Andrews member Patrick Ward-Thomas to describe the possibility of violation of the sacred soil. Indeed all the Golf links of Scotland have been treated as inviolable, each blade of grass to be reverenced, no clot lofted unseen. But it was from St. Andrews that Golf spread to all parts of the world where the earth was no object. Scottish missionaries found no terrain too impassable, no native too hostile, for the building of a clubhouse in the image of the Temple.

The British Empire was won by the English but was secured by the Scots, who followed up the explorers with the Golf courses that totally subdued the natives. In North America the savage manhood rites of the Indians paled into mere inconvenience when the aboriginals observed the white man inflicting upon himself the torment of Golf. In Africa, tribes that might have resisted the cross and the cannon gave up, cowed, at the sight of the implacable Scottish Golfer

Why the cliffs of Dover turned white

wading into a snake-infested swamp to retrieve his ball. Mad dogs and Englishmen went out in the noonday sun, but the Golfer did it with a cumbersome pack on his back, in heat that would stun a camel.

Is there a connection between the Scotsman's natural talent for money management—notably as head of the Bank of England—and the Golfization of much of the planet? Absolutely. Golf is an upper-caste faith. The meek may inherit the earth, but they will still have to play on the public Golf course. The private Golf and Country Club is the only course that matters, in the eyes of the Supreme Being (the Professional Golfers Association), which adheres to the belief that many are called but few are chosen by the membership committee.

Poor countries that have never known the blessing of a Scot as minister of finance have few Golf courses. They use the land to plant rice or graze cattle, a tragic waste. Their rich people must go abroad to practice Golf, thus reducing domestic supplies of humility. Such, at least, is the Golfer's doctrine. Let us examine in the cold light of science his premise that the nation is mistaken that beats its swords into plowshares, instead of wedges.

37

38

41

This Vale of Tees

Dog's-leg

Golfer, new to the club, stands on the first tee and swings at the ball. He misses. He swings again. Again he misses. And again. "God!" he exclaims. "This sure is a tough course."

(Old Golf joke)

No two Golf courses are exactly alike. God gives us the snowflakes, of which each is unique, but the Golf course comes from the Devil, to show the infinitely various forms of evil. A person who plays tennis, or football, or basketball, knows that each court or field

Communing with nature

will have the same lines and dimensions. Because he is merely playing a game, he accepts this uniformity of rectangular space without feeling emotionally starved. Not so the Golfer.

For the Golfer the course, in itself, is something to be overcome. He does not require competition from other human beings in order to be beaten. He is reduced to quivering despair by a tree, a molehill, a babbling brook that is out-babbled by the owner of the ball that has landed in it. For thousands of years, man has loved the beauty in nature. The Golfer discovers a way to hate it. A Golfer can look at a grove of graceful poplars and see only a leafy monster, barring his progress to the green. Narcissus gazed upon his reflection in a pool and became so infatuated with his own image that he took root as a beautiful flower. In contrast, the Golfer whose ball lies in the pond catches a glimpse of the mirrored expression on his face and he seeds the area with poison ivy.

To summarize: many religions find God in every aspect of nature; the Golfer finds Him in the bar.

Designing of the Golf course goes back, in spirit, to

Zen and the art of Golf

the Labyrinth of Crete. That maze was built to accommodate the monstrous Minotaur, which had the head of a bull and the body of a man. All subsequent Golf courses have been laid out with the bull-headed man in mind. The maze itself, however, has been cunningly refined from a simple complex of dead ends into today's masterpiece of contrived nemesis. Let us examine its components, remembering that any one of them is potent enough to evoke hysteria in a yak.

The Tee

Just as Golf has two meanings for the word *club*, it has two meanings for *tee*. (It also has two meanings for *balls*, depending on which zipper the Golfer plays with.) *Tee* can mean (a) the relatively small, flat place from which the Golfer sets forth, or backward, depending on the flight (if any) of his first shot; or (b) the peg, worm turd, or other prop on which the ball is set in the mistaken belief that this will make it easier to hit. Under normal rules the Golfer may place his ball on the tee, but not off the tee. That is, he must be on the tee before he can put his ball on the tee, unless he prefers not to put his ball on the tee, in which case he may be anywhere (along with the damned, elusive Pimpernel).

Off the tee, the Golfer may put his ball on the tee only if winter rules are in effect. The Golfer who thinks of himself as a man for all seasons will tee up any time no one is looking. He is beneath contempt. The true

Gypsy tee room

Golfer will not tee up on the fairway till the frost is on the pumpkin. In fact he may play the pumpkin instead of the ball. Much depends on what he has been drinking to keep warm. One of the tests of manhood, for the Golfer, is trying to find a tee in his pocket when his hands are frozen. Some Golfers have hurt themselves rather badly, groping for a tee that wasn't there.

Even more hazardous to health is the tee into which the tee is inserted. The common form is a raised altar, reminiscent of that on which the Aztecs

Tee for two

performed human sacrifice. This tee may be either grass or artificial matting, depending on whether the self-destruction is private or public. The tee for the Great Unwashed found on public driving ranges, where the rabble are content with any rude platform on which to dispatch their bucket of balls, usually has a surface of fibre or striated rubber resistant enough to

the little peg to escalate a minor back problem into a permanent right angle. To avoid the embarrassment of being carried off the tee in this missionary position, some older Golfers use a very tall peg, or have their legs shortened, whichever seems the better investment.

The limits of a grass tee are generally designated

by a pair of round objects—rocks, human skulls, whatever suits the character of the course. As the grass becomes chopped up by flailing clubs, the markers are moved, the process being repeated till it is manifest that as a defoliant the Golfer is almost as safe as Agent Orange.

The tee is also the place where the Golfer answers the call of nature (the tee-pee). Because the course takes him so far away from indoor plumbing, and the round may last as long as five hours, all but the most continent Golfer must seek sanctuary in the bush surrounding a tee. This is why for so many years Golf remained a monastic order. The presence of women at the tee, either in the male Golfer's own foursome or in that waiting, greatly complicates his finding an excuse for absenting himself from the assembly. Deliberately driving one's ball into the rough seems a high price to pay. Yet contrived utterances such as "Excuse me, I think I see a rare species of mushroom behind that thicket," or "I like to meditate alone in the woods before attempting this hole" fool no one. Especially when the adjacent scene is suddenly supplemented by what sounds, to the perpetrator at least, like Niagara Falls in freshet.

Women Golfers who protest about being given separate times to play do not understand that men Golfers are mainly protecting themselves from being charged with indecent exposure. Mixed Golf has indeed sharpened the ordeal of the game in that untold numbers of male Golfers have had to learn the virtue of

Stylite

Pro-state problem

silence in letting it run down the leg. The only ones smiling are those catheterized and confident that they have their tinkle, so to speak, in the bag.

So much for the tee as religious retreat. If all goes well, after this cloistered interval, the Golfer sets forth on the most positive part of the course (for those fortunate enough to find it).

The Fairway

The straight and narrow. This is the moral significance of the fairway in Golf. It materializes the path of righteousness, for the benefit of people who lose interest in it after dark.

Fairways vary in quality, from mere resurrected pasture to fescues as soigné as a whore's hair-do. Like Life itself, the fairway lies so invitingly before the Golfer that it is inconceivable that his ball should seek any other avenue to consummation. Alas, reality awaits. The ball, having had a decent home life and been struck only when deserving, should fly high and true two-hundred-fifty yards down the middle of the fairway. Instead it is seized in mid-flight by evil powers that convince it that the deviate is an alternate lifestyle.

It then curves off the fairway, gleefully, to left or to right, to plummet into the woods. It ricochets off tree trunks (the crack of doom). A crow caws derision. Then, silence. Except for his opponent's upturned gaze, the Golfer sees nothing to indicate that his effort has changed the world for the better, or in fact that he has had any previous existence at all. Instead he has become an instant leper. He walks into the wilderness, figuratively ringing a little bell and mumbling "Unclean . . . unclean . . ." Spurning the fairway, his ball has landed in the Golfer's nightmare:

The Rough

The rough is a bordering stretch of vegetation that may be the habitat of many forms of venomous creature besides the Golfer looking for his ball. When a snake bites a Golfer in the rough, it is generally the snake that dies.

Some Golf courses have no rough to speak of. The Golfer's errant ball lands on the adjoining fairway, where it is played by a Golfer headed in the opposite direction. On the roughless course it is not unusual for the Golfer to have his ball drop at his feet five minutes after he hit it. This heightens his awareness of trying to contend with powers beyond his understanding.

For a full spiritual life, the Golfer must face the rough as forest primeval . . .

> Only God can make a tree,
> A tree that may in Summer wear
> A nest of robins in her hair,
> A tree that's girdled like a monk,
> A Golfer's club wrapped 'round her trunk.

The compleat rough

"Yes, Bambi, hunting is cruel."

The denser the rough, the greater the opportunity afforded the Golfer for meditation. Away from the hurly-burly of civilization, he has these precious moments to be alone with his thoughts. All the complex problems of computerized living are reduced to one simple task: finding his ball. His is the child's delight in the Easter egg hunt. For this reason the ideal rough is sufficiently primitive to provide unlimited hiding places for the ball, yet is not so impenetrable that the Golfer yields to excess, clawing shrubs out of the ground with his bare hands and growling at anyone who attempts to remove the fir cone from his mouth.

At its best, the rough is a test of the Golfer's resolve to live in harmony with nature, or at least to move it away from his ball. The manner in which the Golfer conducts his search in the rough says much about his character. If he proceeds like King Kong responding to the teeing up of Fay Wray, toppling sizable trees and leaving all plant life flattened in his wake, the Golfer may not be altogether adjusted to the ecosystem. He has the soul of a developer. But if the Golfer treats the rough with respect, treading lightly through the bracken, restoring each twig to its bent, he enjoys inner peace. Either that or he is AWOL from the Enchanted Forest.

Poison ivy, toxic spiders, wood ticks—all these help to enrich the rough experience. Even where the undergrowth has been cleared out, to leave only a solitary oak, the Golfer's imagination is such that he at

Mashie Niblick wading in a Cleek with divining Brassie

once assumes that (a) the tree harbours a squirrel which, mistaking the ball for an albino walnut, picked it up from the fairway and hid it in the tree; or (b) the ball dropped into a knothole, the oak being a nympho-maniac; or (c) the tree is a mirage induced by thirst. The Golfer who spends a great deal of time communing with the rough is easy to identify—his teeth are covered with pine needles. Only if he persists in delaying the game, however, by dancing about playing the pipes of Pan, with a garland of wildflowers in his hair, should he be declared unplayable.

Other Hazards

Irresistible attraction though it is (cf. Putney Flubb's *1001 Things to Do in the Rough*), the lunatic fringe of the Golf course is but part of the game's contribution to complete mental breakdown. Consider, for example, the *dogleg*.

None but the brave deserve the fairway: that is the lesson taught by the dogleg. The dogleg is in fact a morality play. The theme: is it more blessed modestly to skirt the leg, though this take several strokes, or to risk perdition with one bold blow that flouts the canine femur? In terms of valour, the dogleg defines the Golfer. For is it not written that Life itself is a dogleg? If we could all see the flag from the tee, how much easier it would be to hole out in regulation!

Circumvention doth make cowards of us all. And the dogleg invites discretion, the timid tacking into the

Casual water

wind that blows away all hope of promotion. The dogleg discriminates against not only the coward but also left-handers, women, and people too near-sighted to notice that the green is not visible. The Golfer doesn't care. He devoutly believes that the well-designed course offers enough different kinds of adversity to deny survival of the fittest, and to bring the eagle to earth with the chicken.

One of these trials is *the water hazard*. The water hazard is of two kinds: *casual water* and *nervous water*. Casual water usually takes the form of a puddle. The puddle may be man-made, in which case

Aloha links

A game for all seasons

the player should remove his ball from it as quickly as possible. There is no penalty attached to casual water, unless it reaches flood proportions and carries the Golfer out to sea.

Nervous water, however, is a stream or pond or river or lake or, in California, the Pacific Ocean. The compleat Golf course must have nervous water. It is cruel and unnatural to expect the Golfer to play eighteen holes of Golf without having the means whereby to drown himself. Even though the creek or pond comes up only to his hips, so long as he can see his ball the

Golfer will find a way to join it on the bottom. St. Andrew, it will be remembered, was a fisherman. In a very real sense the Golfer is returning to his spiritual origins when, having driven his ball straight into the eminently obvious body of water between him and the hole, he casts his net for that which is not given unto him, though he cast himself in with it.

Some Golf courses, particularly in Africa, feature a tree house built near the water hole, so that visitors may have a blind from which to observe the Golfer when he comes to the water hole for his ball. This is tasteless voyeurism. Although the Golfer's antics in fishing for his ball are often hilarious, an enraged Golfer can be extremely dangerous. The popular belief that Golfers can't climb trees is simply not true. The water hole should be treated with the respect due the one aqueous environment known to terrify piranha.

Also testing the Golfer's temper is *the sand trap*. The dictionary accurately defines the sand trap as a depression containing sand. The depression grows with each stroke. It gradually deepens from a manic depression to the pit of despair. The sand trap is thus without doubt the most exquisitely tortuous hazard that Golf can offer to try the will to live. Although bunker jokes are common ("He has spent more time in the sand than Rommel"), no Golfer escapes the stark symbolism of the trap. In the midst of green pastures, he has found the wasteland. He alone stands in an oasis of grief. Like the anchorite he has sought out the desert, there to purge his soul of all earthly hope.

Sand traps guarding the green commonly have the shape of a kidney. This kidney, like that in the human body, removes impurities—such as poise and grace—from the Golfer's spirit. There is no mistaking the club member who spends most of his leisure time in the bunker: his face shines with the special clean of the sand-blasted. He may also be able to swivel his eyeballs independently of one another. In extreme cases the Golfer has been seen to dig a hole in the sand with his hind flippers, drop a clutch of balls into the

Executive sandbox

hole and cover them up, apparently in the expectation that they will hatch.

Occasionally the Golfer will find something lying in the sand trap, other than another Golfer. He must then ask himself whether his ball is obstructed by a *loose impediment*. A loose impediment is a natural object, such as a stone that can be picked up without a crowbar, a leaf, a beetle (the insect, not the car), or the victim of a heart attack. It may be moved without penalty unless the loose impediment is in a hazard, such as a sand trap or a lake. The Golfer whose ball has landed beside a couple making love in the rough may not ask the couple to move unless one of them is smoking a cigar (an artificial object). The loose impediment is the cause of much soul-searching among sensitive Golfers. Stricken with guilt after moving an apple core to play out of a bunker, the Golfer can become a *tight impediment*. He may be moved out of the club bar without penalty.

These are the main physical hazards of the Golf course, outside the Act of God (being partnered with a clergyman who doesn't swear). Before leaving the subject, however, we must ask ourselves, and anyone else who will listen: Has today's Golf course become too civilized? As one of the times that try men's souls, should it try harder? A beloved pastor of the game, Father Lee of Trevino, has said that the rough is not what it was, that the water hazards have lost something since they took out the crocodiles. "There is nothing to fear," sayeth the Mexican patriarch. "If you had some big grass out there, you might see their knuckles turn white."

The menace is clear. The Golf course is in danger of becoming a place where people *seek pleasure*. A hyperthyroid pitch 'n' putt. Mere grassy avenues where the long-ball hitter is king, and the ghost of Bobby Jones weeps at the fleshly sight of so many pink knuckles. To the Golf fundamentalist, the faith is imperilled by the permissive Golf course. Hence the growth of that strict religious order that calls for a return to the holy terror of the Gothic links. This concept is reproduced from a recently discovered manuscript by Mary Wollstonecraft Shelley entitled *Frankenstein's Golf Course*. It tells in chilling detail what can happen when a slightly deranged scientist constructs a par-65 monster that ultimately destroys him. An excerpt:

December 24

My experiments are much facilitated since my being joined by the grotesquely ugly and misshapen dwarf I encountered in the woods, near the thirteenth tee. Igor is almost more than a caddy. He has found for me living parts for my project such as I could never have procured on my own from the mail-order catalogue. He is built closer to the ground than I, better able to descry objects, both alive and cadaverous, that I require to build the Golf course that is a living Hell.

December 28

Refreshed by the Christmas break, I am back at work on the bunker. Somewhere Igor found a quarry of round, white stones of precisely the same size as a Golf ball. Glorious! A man could go mad, trying to find his ball in this pit. I shall move it, en masse, to flank my green made of flypaper. My assistant has also unearthed a pale, puff mushroom. When struck by a club, it emits a cloud of spores which, inhaled, immediately affect the Golfer's perception of reality so that he tries to putt standing on his head. I know that God will be pleased.

The white man's burden

January 5

I have completed the delicate operation of grafting the hornets' nest to the underside of the little rustic bridge across the creek on the tenth. Igor has walked—with that horrible, shuffling gait of his—across the little bridge several times, each time being stung and stepping on a board that

73

sprang up and hit him in the face. My labours approach the final judgement.

February 12

At last! Dr. Frankenstein's Golf course is completed! I am ready to show it to the world, as soon as the last snow melts on the quicksand. But first I must test it myself. This very morn I shall set forth with Igor carrying the rubber-shafted clubs that were a last-minute appendage to the brute of a course. (I have rejected the square ball, as a mischievous whisper from the Devil.) Even as I write, I see the buzzards—imported from the Sahara with reckless disregard for expense—circling over the first hole, scenting God knows what carrion. To the tee!

February 13

O God, what have I wrought? Hounds and hags of Hades pursue me! Slashing at me with aerating forks! Igor, my poor little Igor, dead! Devoured by the Venus's flytrap! The plant seemed such a nice touch at the time. But now Igor is gulped, and I stare in frozen horror at my card: 138! And that is only the first hole. I am doomed to feed the monstrous creature, forever. I can hear it growling for its lime, its potash, its top dressing of witch's dung . . .

A tragic tale. Frankenstein was the victim of a splendid vision gone cross-eyed. But he saw that the well-designed Golf course transfigures the celebration of a Black Mass that climaxes with:

The Green

"There's many a slip 'twixt the cup and the lip." This old English proverb, going back to some anonymous Golfer who had just three-putted, says it all about the special contribution of the green to the perversity of Fate. 'Twixt the lip of the green and the cup that cheers rarely: here lie the subtle slips that enable the young and strong to be as thoroughly demoralized as the old and silly.

A cleat clot

Reforestation

In his debatable work *Greens and When to Eat Them*, Putney Flubb interprets the green as a kind of chastity belt. "Five hundred yards of foreplay," he writes, "are frustrated by six inches of failed penetration." This image is simplistic. Granted, it is possible, by stretching the imagination, to conceive of the Golf course as a surrogate for coitus interruptus. But this does not explain the popularity of the game with women, for whom, in the main, there is no sexual connotation to attaining the hole in a minimum of tries.

No, to the mature Golfer the green means more than one of eighteen pubic areas. The green is an emerald isle set in a sea of troubles, only closer inspection proving it to be more treacherous than the deep.

It is not, for instance, flat. A totally horizontal surface surrounding the pocket indicates that the green was designed by someone who had a traumatic experience with a billiard table.

A green without slopes is like a woman without hips: the challenge is not worthy of the effort.

The most estimable greens are those created by experts trained in the midway carnie games in which balls are rolled at holes, with the success rate of a snowball in Hell. It takes a master craftsman to contour the green so that, wherever his ball lands on it, the green brings the Golfer to his knees, squinting to judge the roll of the ball, holding up his putter like St. Joan invoking the saints, plucking imaginary blades of grass from the fancied trajectory of his putt, and generally acting like a surveyor's instrument that has swallowed its plumb line.

> And thus do we of wisdom and of reach,
> With windlasses and with assays of bias,
> By indirections find directions out.
>
> (*Hamlet*, II, i, 64)

Obviously, Polonius knew his greens. His words confirm that, thanks to Golf, the state of Denmark was even more rotten than Hamlet suspected. And like the poison poured into his father's ear, the perfect green paralyses the Golfer completely. He never putts at all. As darkness falls, he is still standing there, crouched over his putter, staring at the cup, then at his ball, then at the cup, then at his ball . . .

Vestments & Paraphernalia

The slice of life

foursome is playing the green beside a highway when a funeral cortège of cars passes. One of the Golfers pauses over his putt, removes his cap and waits respectfully till the hearse has passed. A companion having commented on this courteous observance, the Golfer says: "Well, after all, I was married to the old gal for twenty-five years."

(Old Golf Joke)

As a priesthood, Golf has seduced away from the church thousands of men who don't look good in a dress. In fact, one of the most inviting features of the game is that the Golfer's vestment consists of ordinary trousers and sports shirt. Knobby knees and Rand McNally maps of varicose veins are mercifully hidden from view, and the Golfer's cap is optional, depending on the diocese of the bald spot.

Because Golf is not a contact sport, no special padding is necessary, except in the cell. Golfers who spend an inordinate amount of time on their knees, praying, may choose to reinforce their pants in that area. It was once believed to be unlucky to have the cuffs of the trousers touch the ground, or barbed wire, or other low-lying objects. This led to the development of plus fours. Still worn in remote parts of Britain, such as the Outer Hebrides, plus fours were so called because the loose, tweedy knickers were made four inches longer than standard knickers. They lost favour when Golfers saw plus fours as being ladies' bloomers that had had a sex change. Also, a few Golfers indulged in the excess of plus eights, carrying their clubs in them and disgracing the cloth.

Shorts on a male Golfer are an abomination. Short shorts are doubly damned. A Golfer wearing shorts who attempts to enter a private country club may expect to be stopped by the Swiss Guard, or at least by a club manager with gruyère on his breath. That municipal courses tolerate exposure of the thigh is merely the measure of revelation gone wrong. The

Attitudes of Prayer: (1) Genuflexion

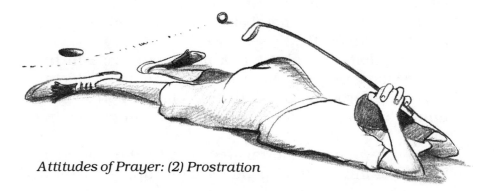

Attitudes of Prayer: (2) Prostration

experiment with Bermuda shorts has been condemned as heresy, even in Bermuda. Only the woman Golfer is permitted a habit which concedes that she has legs. This is a concession to male Golfers—especially those somewhat myopic—who depend on the knee-length skirt to identify the female. Such visual guidance is vital in situations like popping behind a tree to terrorize the ants, or judging how much time the foursome ahead will spend in exchanging recipes. Otherwise, the skirt is asexual. A female Golfer who posed for a magazine wearing provocative lingerie sent a shudder of horror through the Golfing world. The thought of what those spiked heels could do to an innocent green . . .

The entire sole must be spiked. This is the essence of *the Golf shoe*. The danger of losing his grip at the upper end of the body makes it crucial to the Golfer that at least his feet be secure. Ordained Golf shoes ensure *proper stance*, as opposed to *improper stance*, or doing the splits. Golfers who try to cheap it out with sneakers are regarded as a menace to themselves and to their fellow club members, losing traction on hills and blocking traffic.

The Golf shoe also has a paramount role in the confessional of the locker-room. Lacing and unlacing his shoe affords the Golfer the merciful opportunity to unburden his soul to a senior member without having to look him in the eye.

Sins venial and mortal are heard by the Golf shoe. Details of infidelity, impending bankruptcy, prostate

Getting in front of the ball

problems—the cushion support bears an enormous onus. Not surprisingly, it carries so much responsibility that the Golf shoe has gone into analysis. An advertisement in *Golf Digest* for the *de rigueur* shoe advises that it is "the only company that has extensively biomechanically analyzed what happens to your foot during a golf swing." This Golf shoe was biomechanically engineered in the laboratory of "a major state university." One pictures the climactic moment in the lab:

"Eureka!"

"We still have foot odour, Dr. Podney? Despite the revolutionary, built-in sani-liner?"

"No, McFungus! This is *it*! The biomechanical breakthrough we've been working on all these years. Praise be to St. Nicklaus!"

"You mean—?"

"Yes! I've put it on the blackboard. The formula for the ultimate Golf shoe!"

"We've beaten the Russians?"

"By a country foot! I knew it was worth it, all those months of lying on a bed of spikes to get the earthy feel of the shoe."

"It's a proud moment for America, Doctor."

"Yes. If President Eisenhower had waged Golf in this shoe, the Stars and Stripes might still be flying over the Havana Country Club."

Second only to the shoe, a critical part of the Golf habit is *the Golf glove*. To appear on the course with

The club is mightier than the sword

nude hands is intolerable. This breach of decency, if not an indictable offence, is at the very least gross conduct. Lady members are apt to swoon at the sight of a naked, hairy paw wrapped around a Golf club, even if the paw belongs to a man.

Those who don't know better think they can acquire the Golf glove by taking an ordinary pair of old

Shafted clubs

gloves with the fingers out and throwing one of them away. Naive. The Golf glove is a oneness. It symbolizes the monotheism of Golf. Some players refer to it, frivolously, as a swinging single. They are more to be pitied than censured. The Golf glove serves the solemn purpose of swathing the left hand (if the Golfer is right-handed), or the right hand (if the Golfer is left-handed).

Choosing the Right Club: (1) Contemplation

It enables him to tell his hands apart. Once they have become laced in the grip around the shaft of the club, all his fingers look alike. The Golfer may panic, if he thinks his digits are hopelessly entwined. Being able to identify the hand with the glove, however, he feels confident that he can free it at any time, and use it to perform other tasks. A glove treated with alum also discourages thumb-sucking.

Some purists insist that the Golf glove is an affectation, or a psychological crutch for Golfers who live in

Choosing the Right Club: (2) Rejection (Hesitation)

fear of their grip. They are mistaken. The glove goes
back to Elizabethan times. Golf scholars report finding
a folio of Shakespeare's play in which the reason why
Romeo is in Juliet's garden is that he is looking for his
Golf ball. And the Golf glove is clearly alluded to when
Romeo cries "Oh, that I were a glove upon that hand,
that I might touch that cleek!"

However, where Golf stands best revealed by the
splendour of its trappings is with *the set of clubs and
their bag*. These are of a size and opulence usually

Choosing the Right Club: (3) Revelation (Inspiration)

borne by an elephant as evidence of a maharajah's net worth. It is through his clubs that the Golfer displays the magnificence of his obsession.

Yet the Golf club had humble beginnings. The most widely accepted theory is that the modern club was born when an ancient Scot bought a cane because he was lame, then was miraculously cured of his affliction. Too cheap to give up the cane, he reversed it and lashed at small stones to show his gratitude to Providence. This crude implement was quickly improved

Choosing the Right Club: (4) Consummation

upon. Golfers discovered the relationship between the face of the club and the loft of the ball. The Golf course thus became the only place in the world in which a helpless object is subjected to a variety of instruments, outside a hospital operating room. Indeed, one reason why Golf has so many doctors and surgeons among its followers is that it is an extension of putting an unstable body into a hole in the ground.

The early Golf clubs were fashioned entirely of oak by Scotsmen who enjoyed working with wood, but not long enough to risk cutting themselves. This is why there are no Scottish totem poles. What the whittlers did give to the world was the *long spoon*, the *driver* or *play-club*, the *brassy niblick*, and the *putter*. Why did the Scot call it a long spoon? Obviously to fool his neighbours into thinking he was making something to stir a tall drink. For the same reason (the Oppression) nothing is known about the origin of the name of the niblick. One legend has it that the club, designed to winkle the ball out of awkward niches, was created by one Willie McNiblick, when in a towering rage he bit the face off his spoon. In any event, to discourage further attempts to make the game pleasurable, the early Golfers shod the sole of the niblick with brass to make the brassy niblick—the first major step towards the Golf club as inedible.

The transition was completed with the Iron Age. During this period appeared the *lofting iron*, the *mashie*, and the *cleek*. These irons expanded the religious ecstasy of Golf by taking a bigger divot than the wooden-headed club. It is significant that *mashie* is believed to derive from the same French word *(massue)* as *mace*, the name given to the spiked club popular in the Middle Ages for demolition of a foe's armour. The same violent desperation marks the etymology of *cleek*, from the Scottish word *cleken*, to clutch. The cleek was a large iron hook used to suspend a pot over a fire, when not in use to cook one's goose on the course.

Today, when names have been replaced by

Choosing the Right Club: (5) Mortification

numbers up to 10 and more, the angling of the face of the irons is even more subtle. It would in fact be difficult to justify the Golfer's staggering about under their considerable combined weight were it not for a cardinal factor: *they permit the Golfer to blame the club for a poor shot.* In the choice of clubs lies exculpation. Other games, non-secular that they are, afford the player only one implement—tennis racket, hockey stick, cricket bat—to be held accountable. But when the Golfer swings his iron and cuts the ball in half, he is granted the excuse of having chosen the No. 5 iron instead of the No. 4 iron. If he has a caddy to trust in the delicate transmission of the correct club, the possibilities of absolution are infinite. Insofar as choice is the key to spiritual survival, Golf clubs, in their infinite variety, help to mitigate the severeness of Fate. The predeterminist—easily spotted by his carrying only a driver, a mashie, and a putter in a skinny bag—is despised by the orthodox Golfer. In the private club, he may find the tires slashed on his Golf car.

The Golfer who owns a complete set of clubs, however, is universally recognized as a person accustomed to making decisions. Each decision may take long enough to be mistaken for catalepsy, but this is what makes Golf one of the great contemplative religions. Other sport is mere action. Impulse is rife. If the player makes a bad judgement in propelling the ball or puck, in a matter of seconds he has the chance to make another bad judgement. Golf, in contrast, thanks to the plenitude of sources for nothing happening, is a kind of inspired inertia. All but the blind or importunate see a poetry in the slow withdrawal of the club from the bag, the gazing at the horizon, the return of the club to the bag, the withdrawal of another club from the bag . . . There is good reason why the senior executive feels free to practise chip shots in his office. His associates recognize that it is not just play but preparation for corporate life, in which poise counts for more than action.

Before we leave the subject of the clubs, we must

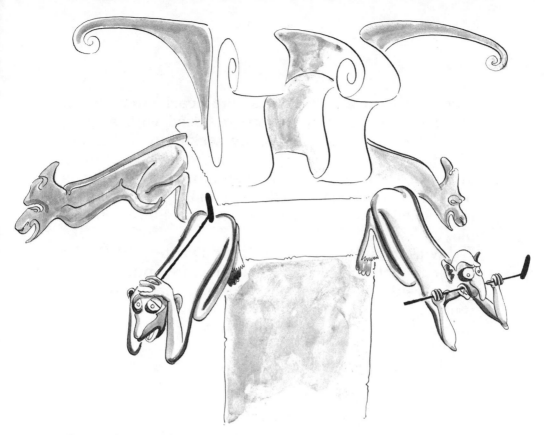

Gargoyles—Cathedral of the Perpetual Putt

acknowledge that which is the most personal and occult of them all: *the putter*. The Golfer may be casual about how he chooses a spouse, but his putter must be right. The putter can be flat or bulbous, cantilevered, goose-necked, duck-tailed, weighted and shafted to be assembled like a billiard cue, so that the Golfer may pack it in a suitcase and travel anywhere in the world without fear of being trapped alone in a hotel room.

Putters are available with a built-in protractor that

reads the green and indicates, like a carpenter's level, the exact direction of the stroke. Used with a heat-sensing ball that automatically seeks out the caddy standing behind the flag, this putter reduces putting to an exact science. For this reason anyone using it is treated as a Golf scientologist, and may have his putter introduced to a hole that even Arnold Palmer never played.

With today's beautifully crafted putter, the Golfer has complete assurance that his three-putting the green results exclusively from his own ineptitude. The putter certifies the primacy of human error. On such foundation Golf builds the sturdy spires of manic depression.

Even more awesome than the putter is *the Golf bag*. Over the eons the Golf bag has developed from a simple quiver, with diameter scarcely more than that of a man's arm, to the capacious and elegant accom-modation of today. With the shrinking of the dimen-sions of the automobile, the familiar exercise of tossing the Golf bag into the car is being reversed. The older Golfer, taking advantage of soaring real estate values, plans to sell his home and retire into his Golf bag. Like the hermit crab, he can enjoy the security of a shell not his own, the original occupant having died. If he is particularly nomadic, the Golfer will put his huge Golf bag and clubs into a moulded travel case, of which one advertisement says "truly a suit of armour for all your golf equipment." The total weight of this panoply strikes terror into the heathen (hotel porters, redcaps, chambermaids). But, like the sea tortoise, if the Golfer carrying his bag is flipped on his back he is helpless. Unless righted, he will die in the sun, his limbs flailing feebly, a tragic victim of his own bulwark.

The hand cart was created as a conveyance that the Golfer could collapse before he did. It resulted in The Great Schism. The puritan fathers of Golf rejected the cart as reducing the Golfer to a draught animal. The Golf bag rides in majesty, while the rickshaw boy

Normal attitude, mixed pairs

99

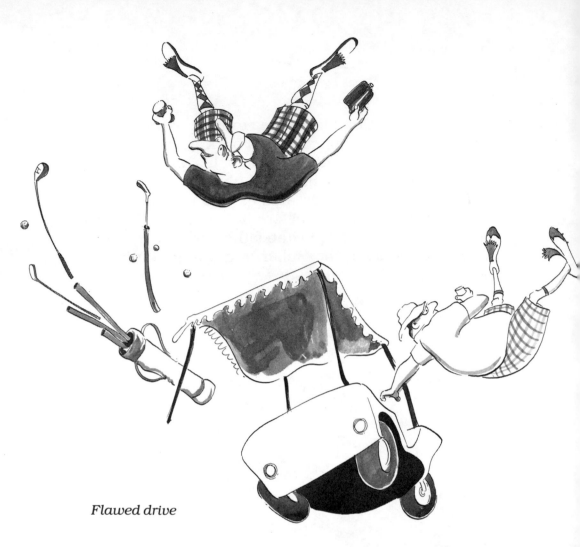

Flawed drive

hauling it struggles up hills, and on down slopes is sometimes run over by his own carriage—shades of the Hindu Juggernaut.

The Great Schism has widened with the coming of *the Golf car*. These electric vehicles, used mostly by private-club members, accelerate the movement of the Golfer to his ball, or where he thinks his ball is. This

Every man shall bear his own burden

leads to inevitable conflict with the Golfer on foot. His progress stalled, the Golf car driver demands that the pedestrian Golfer be restricted to a sidewalk along the fairway, with fines for jaywalking. This campaign to develop fairway into freeway sparked The Walkers' Revolt (1982).

Some observers link The Walkers' Revolt with the

general return to traditional values dating from the election of Ronald Reagan to the U.S. presidency. Others point out that it is cheaper to recharge the battery of the walking Golfer—assuming that he has a hearing aid—than to rent a Golf car. Whatever the spark, the rebellion of the Golfers using shank's mare led to bitter confrontation with the mobile units humming hatred of the infantry. There occurred several ugly incidents in which foot Golfers holed up in bunkers, daring a dune buggy to open fire.

Those Golfers leading The Walkers' Revolt know that this holy war must be won, if the Golf faith is to preserve the asceticism that in the beginning was adopted as an attractive alternative to giving up food and drink. But the battle is far from won. Many younger Golfers have never walked in their lives. They can jog, or skate, or ski, but the aerobic mechanics of ambulation are something they must be taught, preferably by a professional. Once a young Golfer has learned to walk sideways, like a crab, or, worse, backwards, he is extremely difficult to retrain.

The walking Golfers face powerful forces that will stop at nothing, including traffic lights. The headquarters of the Golf car Mafia is of course the Golf links of Las Vegas. That the state of Nevada legalized gambling and prostitution is venial compared to the Mob's enforcing use of the Golf car by taking the recalcitrant for a slow ride, deep-sixing them in the 18th lake.

The most capricious among the Golfer's ritual

Improving the lie

objects is *the ball*. The Golfer rarely associates with the same ball long enough to create a meaningful relationship. This is the main difference between a Golf ball and a bowling ball. No matter how badly he propels his ball, the bowler rarely loses it altogether. Some Golfers refuse to admit that their ball is gone forever. They reject assistance in looking for their ball. They want to be alone in this moment of loss. They then find their ball, miraculously, not in the deep rough where it appeared headed but on the edge of the fairway. This is the work of the Golf-ball Fairy. Although no Golfer ever speaks of the Golf-ball Fairy, for fear of frightening her away, this wood nymph is tacitly credited with a wide variety of deeds that *improve the lie*. Without her, the lie would be unimproved to the point of gross prevarication. A touch of the wand removes even the slightest hint of fibbing. The Golfer is able to play the ball without taking the two-stroke penalty that befalls those who don't believe in Tinkerball.

Tinkerball cannot, unfortunately, rescue the ball that lands in a lake or river with a splash clearly visible to the Golfer's companions. Some Golfers carry in their bag a telescopic scoop with which they try to dredge their ball out of the muck, but their efforts merely sharpen the speculation of a pair of visitors from an alien planet observing the spectacle below their saucer . . .

"See, Blobsk, the earthling has driven the round object into the lake."

"Clearly it is some kind of purification rite, Waftch. A substitute for giving his belongings to the poor."

"Now he takes another of the white eggs from the mother bag. How carefully he sets it on the little stick! He greatly cares about its welfare. Now he swings his club . . . ah, again his treasure lands in the water."

"How happy he is to have simplified his life by divesting himself of material possession! See, he weeps with joy."

"Wait, the round objects cannot be eggs after all. They are nuts. Why else would the earthling be banging his head against the trunk of the tree? He seeks to shake loose more fruit with which to propitiate the lake."

"Perhaps the lake is inhabited by some god that must be appeased. Could that be the celebrated Loch Ness? To get safely past the monster in the loch they must project the albino meatballs into its lair?"

"I think not, Blobsk. The earthling just threw himself into the lake as well."

Despite the transient nature of the Golf ball, the ball incorporates much that symbolizes evil for the Golfer. (It is significant that the professional Golfer, as his first gesture after winning a tournament, hurls his ball as far away from him as he can.) Every Golfer knows that beneath that fair, dimpled complexion lie components of the satanic, layering a lethal core. At its centre the Golf ball is a microcosm of the planet's infernal regions—cold magma roiling and seething in demoniac rage as the ball, like Beelzebub, is cast down from heaven into the everlasting slough.

The old theological debate about the number of angels that can dance on the head of a pin is replaced, among Golfers, by learned discussion of the aerodynamically optimum number of pits on the ball. Next to a blameless life, the Golfer yearns most for a seamless ball whose flight is as inexorable as that of Archangel Michael. A few Golfers push their ball superstition to the extreme. They believe that the inevitability of losing their ball on the first drive depends on how new the ball is. A brand new ball, fresh from the cellophane, won't even make it out of the clubhouse. A battered repaint, however, will land in the middle of the fairway, if for no other reason than to draw attention to the fact that its owner is cheap. In an attempt to outwit this fiendish scenario, Golfers switch balls from new to old and back to new as often as possible during the round. They hope to confuse the fates.

Besides the perfect Golf ball, the religious journals of Golf advertise a variety of charms: personalized tees, mural-sized reproductions of paintings of famous Golf courses, pack bottles for the sacramental wine. The knitted headcover for the woods is frowned on by most private clubs. There was a period when the woolly bonnets were tolerated as a bit of comic relief in the generally spartan tone of the Golf bag. But indulgence led to excesses (pom-poms, "happy" faces, and crocheted names such as Eenie, Meenie, Miney and Moe). Today, to avoid being suspected of having a frivolous attitude towards the game, the Golfer hoods his clubs in plain leather jackets consecutively numbered (No. 13 optional). The covers should be held on by elasticized necks, as the sound of the zipper can distract other Golfers, particularly ladies' fours.

Rites & Mysteries

Opening the face

¶ *Golfer returned home late from his round and told his wife: "A dreadful thing happened. I was on the seventh fairway with Charlie, my dear old golf buddy, when a ball hit him on the head and killed him. My God it was terrible—from then on it was hit the ball...drag Charlie...hit the ball...drag Charlie..."*

(Old Golf joke)

The Sweet Sounds of Golf: (1) "Shank!"

The rites of Golf are sometimes divided into two main practices: the processional, or first nine, and the recessional, or back nine. This is silly. A small percentage of Golfers hold to the belief that God created the outward nine in order to raise the hopes that are destroyed on the backward nine. But their fatalism is dismissed as superstition by the majority of Golfers, who see both nines as inspiring equally thoughts of self-destruction.

The Sweet Sounds of Golf: (2) "Scuff!"

Much more relevant to the Golfer's credo is his concept of Time. Non-Golfers think of Time as a continuum, with no substance. The Golfer, however, begins the entire ceremonial of his game by "getting a time." To get a time is as solemn a ritual as removing the shoes before entering a Moslem mosque. In the private Golf club, the most visible part of the caste system is the elevating of those members who have a

The Sweet Sounds of Golf: (3) "Pow!"

time over those who do not. They who do not have a time are Golf's untouchables. On a busy weekend morning they may be seen milling about pitifully, near the pro shop, pretending to have a time when in fact they are timeless. Many never proceed beyond the practice putting green. Others get on the course only after darkness has fallen, playing by flashlight and completing their round in time to see other untouchables teeing off at dawn. They are mocked by the crows and tormented by mosquitoes.

"Getting a time" is therefore one of the most significant factors in the hierarchy of the Golf club. Whether the Golfer has his secretary phone the pro shop for a

The Sweet Sounds of Golf: (4) "Chirp! Peep! Curse!"

time, or trusts no one but himself with such a delicate intercourse with the temporal power, the Golfer learns that to him that hath is it given. Regardless of his other achievements in life, if the only tee-off time he can get, week after week, is 0540 hours, then he is as camel dirt. He is forced into the defensive posture of telling fellow members that he prefers to tee off at sunrise, "with nobody in front of me." Although either of the bags under his eyes is capacious enough to accommodate his set of clubs, he regales the locker-room with comments such as "You haven't played golf till you've seen the greens shimmering with the dew of morn." In point of fact this Golfer is so used to stumbling around the course in morning fog, his cart is equipped with radar. He is afraid of short shadows. He squishes off the last hole, trousers soaked to the knees, just as those with the prime time are taking their first practice swings. He is, literally, small time.

At the other, favoured extreme is the Brahmin who not only gets the most coveted tee-off time, but may hold it in perpetuity. When he dies, he bequeathes it "...and to my dear son, Jock Junior, the ownership of the corporation, my city and country estates, and my 9:30 tee-off time at the club."

The curious thing about this time element in Golf's pecking order is that it does not prevent the situation it was originally intended to avoid, namely a crowd scene of Golfers waiting to step onto the first tee. Private and public courses alike present this spectacle to the Golfer, who must make his first shot before a large gallery whose only good wish for him is that he hits the ball far enough to get the hell out of the way.

How the Golfer deals with this assembly of witnesses, whose charitable feelings towards him are roughly on a par with those of the hags knitting in the shadow of Madame Lafarge in La Place de la Concorde, can determine his future. If he is too shy and nervous to be able to ignore the watchers, and has to be led to the tee wearing blinkers, he is clearly not executive material.

Other Golfers affect a bravado, swaggering onto the tee as if it were the stage of a Vegas casino hotel. There is a good reason why professional entertainers

114

Losing concentration (or: Till Golf do us part)

such as Bob Hope are prominent in Golf. They are accustomed to playing to an audience. (Johnny Carson has introduced many "Tonight" shows holding a Golf club, as a talisman against stage fright.) Indeed it is difficult to judge whether they are Golfers because they are comedians, or comedians because they have played Golf. Whichever, the Golfer who tries to clown his way past the first tee, without help from a team of writers, is courting disaster. Golf is not mocked. The wise Golfer leaves his levity in the locker-room. His watchers will not be charmed by the feat of a little patter.

The most excruciating thing that can happen to the Golfer performing before the crowd waiting at the first tee is of course to miss the ball completely. Not only does he look absurd, but he is delaying the game. For this reason some Golfers lose all sense of propriety and pretend to be taking practice swings, till they actually make contact with the ball. The ethics of the practice swing would fill a volume on their own, but nowhere is the abuse of foreplay more disreputable than on the tee.

The unwritten rule is that the Golfer may take a few practice swings, standing some distance from the ball, before stepping up to it and committing himself to the stroke that counts. However, some Golfers, particularly the old and very crafty ones, master the sly art of appearing to be standing back from the ball when instead they have merely shortened their grip on the club. They take swings, gradually letting the club out till the club strikes the ball. The poker face that the Golfer maintains during this manoeuvre is worthy of a Mississippi riverboat gambler.

On the fairway it is even easier to mask the fanned shot. A common tactic is to keep flailing away at thin air, at the same time shouting "You bleeping mud wasp! Get away from me!" Flying or hopping insects, dandelion seed, low cloud—any of these imagined

Ménage à trois

intrusions may be blamed for the fit of club swinging after the initial whiff. Indeed, in some foursomes the Golfer who admits to having missed the ball is viewed as something of a wimp, lacking in creative imagination. As in all religious art, truth is fact given higher form.

At the other extreme is the Golfer who is at pains to take his practice swings well away from the ball. He may even leave the course. This type of player is a nuisance to other Golfers who pick up any ball not accompanied by an adult. A Golfer should never absent himself from his ball unless he has just hit it.

Verbally, however, Golf is *an honourable game.* The player is on his honour to count each stroke. Some cynics suggest that the main reason why Golf is so popular is that it is the only game where each player is personally responsible for keeping accurate score. The only other sport that places comparable trust in the individual's accountancy is fishing, third place going to sex.

Because the Golfer, like Brutus, is an honourable man, he is said to "have the honour" to tee off first. If the player is a member of the judiciary, a companion says "It's your honour, your honour." The speaker may be an honorary member of the club. Golf is in fact so immersed in the honourable that one readily understands why the Japanese—supremely deferential to honour as they are—have become avid Golfers. The Japanese Golfer has added to the game the ceremony of choosing the correct iron with which to commit hara-kiri. Loss of face, or worse the whole club head, carries the penalty of jumping into a live volcano.

The protocol of Golf is subtle. It involves much more than being able to mark down on the score card an 8 that looks like a 3. The Golfer, like the Hindu mystic, must focus an enormous amount of concentration in order to transcend reality. This means that when one's opponent is into his backswing, one should not pass wind. It also precludes coughing, sneezing, wheezing, snapping bubble gum, tummy rumbles, and reciting the Gettysburg address. The Golfer addressing the ball is aware not only of such sounds but of where his companions are standing. If the rest of his foursome are bunched directly behind his ball, or assume the foetal position with their backs

Improved Instant Lesson: (1) Extending the swing

to the tee, the Golfer is reminded that his drive tends to be erratic. More cruel yet is for his opponent to stand directly in the projected line of flight, as the safest place to be.

The honourable position for the attendant Golfer is to be unobtrusive without making it a major production. Many Golfers, with no other claim to extrasensory perception, can tell when someone behind them is crossing himself. This telepathic sensitivity is especially apparent in the female Golfer. Because she can hear what a man is thinking, there is no safe place in the vicinity of a woman playing Golf unless she has had a lobotomy.

However, the Golfer's worst enemy is his own body. His swing—the soul of his Golf game—may be ruined by any part of his body except that usually blamed for perdition. Head, shoulders, elbows, hands, hips, knees, and feet—any of these, alone or in combination, may be the malefactor. The young Golfer is sometimes blessed with what is called "a natural swing," but he soon learns that innocence is something to be lost, along with his Golf ball. He becomes aware of his body. If he is slow to notice the diabolical nature of his limbs and joints, his fellow Golfers do not hesitate to point out the turpitude lurking in the cock of the wrist, the twist of the neck. By the time he is a mature Golfer, the player has developed a spastic hack at the ball that shows his effort to dissociate himself from his own anatomy. He has heard or read the instructions of Golf pros, telling him to imagine various medieval devices to drive the evil spirits from his body:

> I suggested she imagine a rope connecting her
> right hip to her left knee. If she turned
> correctly, on the backswing, the rope would
> pull her left knee away from the target, weight
> would shift to the right and she would be in
> position to use her lower body more effectively
> on the downswing.
>
> *Golf Digest*

Improved Instant Lesson:
(2) Keeping eyes directly over putting line

Improved Instant Lesson: (3) Controlling backswing

Improved Instant Lesson: (4) Shifting the weight

Improved Instant Lesson:
(5) Relaxing the grip

Some other cruel restraints that Golfers have been urged to imagine are illustrated on pages 119 to 124 (parental guidance is recommended). Sexologists have claimed to find sado-masochistic elements in the token bondage phantasied by the Golfer. But S & M figures in the imaginings of only a minute percentage of Golfers. By far the greater number simply want to dismember themselves, as a firm lesson to their appendages. Unfortunately, quite a few sustain permanent damage. The Golfer who has spent years imagining that his head is locked in a vise finds that he is unable to release it, till someone turns his right ear.

All these submissions to pain are made in quest of *improvement*. Regardless of the moral squalor he tolerates in his other activities, the Golfer is constantly seeking to improve his Golf. He may do so by taking lessons. The lessons never improve his Golf, but they do provide him with additional advice to give to other Golfers, who will also fail to benefit from it. One of the most venerable shibboleths of improvement is "Keep your left arm straight." Golfers have been telling one another to keep their left arm straight for so many hundreds of years that evolutionary mutation has occurred in some of their young, born without a left elbow. This has not improved their Golf, and being able to bend only one elbow has also impaired their performance on the 19th hole.

Besides keeping the left arm straight, Golfers who have taken lessons, or have listened to Golfers who have taken lessons, offer other magic formulas:

- Put all the weight on the right foot, then lift the foot.
- Take a very, very slow backswing. (This lulls the ball into a false sense of security.)
- Follow through with the nose.
- Grip a grapefruit with your chin. Place an egg under your left armpit. Put a cucumber between your legs. If your Golf doesn't improve, you can always open a produce store.

Lesser means of influencing the flight of the ball include:

Washing the ball. To some Golfers, cleanliness is next to Golfiness. At every tee the Golfer takes his ball to the font and laves it vigorously to remove grass stain. The rite goes beyond making the ball visible from a distance. It is an act of purification. The baptismal Golfer wants to scrub everything in sight. He has difficulty hiring a caddy.

Auguries of wind. Ever sensitive to the elements, the Golfer can detect wind where the ordinary mortal would swear the air is dead calm. He knows that the slightest breeze can distort direction or distance. A black, whirling funnel moving towards him at more than 100 m.p.h. affects his choice of club. To determine the direction and velocity of the wind, the Golfer picks up a blade of grass, holds it high, and allows it to fall to the ground. He carefully notes any aberration from the vertical. It is a simple act of divination. Yet it

Allowing for a breeze

never fails to impress the novitiate, who is apt to get carried away and fling handfuls of grass into the air, in severe cases burying and composting himself.

From reading the wind it is an easy step for the Golfer to believe that he can control it. Ulysses received the winds in a leather bag from Aeolus, King of the Wind. Was it a Golf bag? If so, it helps explain why Ulysses had a relatively easy time of it on the odyssey.

Body English:
(1) Statement of intent

Thunder and lightning storms. More Golfers are
killed by bolts of lightning than any other religious
sect. They refuse to view it as criticism. Some have
been struck by lightning more than once, yet they
continue to swear that their scorecard is accurate.
There is no doubt that the number of storm-related
casualties among Golfers would be lower if the Golfer
did not take shelter under the only tree in the vicinity.

When the tree is struck by a thunderbolt and topples on the Golfer, he is often unplayable.

Once the Golfer has paid for the eighteen holes and waited to get on the course, it takes a major catastrophe of nature to force him to abandon his round. One of the concerns of civil defence authorities in Hawaii is that there may occur a volcanic eruption near one of the islands' many Golf courses, the molten ash catching and petrifying forever hundreds of people who thought they had time to putt out.

Body English:
(2) Popular support

Body English: (3) Desires extension of term

Body English: (4) Retraction of original statement

Body English: (5) Fall from grace

Body English: (6) Expletives deleted

Body English. By far the most positive proof that Golf is a largely psychic experience is body English. Several other games—lawn bowling, croquet, the tango—employ body English to influence balls in their movement, but none has raised it to the state of an art, as has Golf. The choreography is often as intricate as an African rain dance. Older Golfers, in particular, commonly perform an impressive repertoire of gyrations, kicks, head-tilts, and incantations ("Get up! Get up!", "Sit down! Sit down!"). The belief in psychokinesis (PK) as an elemental power in Golf is found in professional and amateur alike. PK explains why the ball crawls out of the sandtrap, jumps free of the rough, or swims to the shore of the lake. These parapsychological phenomena occur too frequently in Golf to be called miracles. But they do prove that necromancy is alive and well and living at Pebble Beach.

Scoring & Other Myths

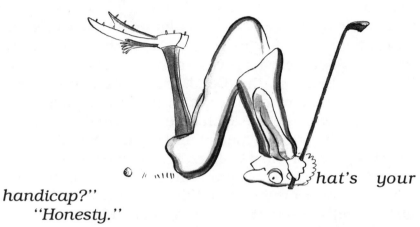

"What's your handicap?"
"Honesty."

(Old Golf joke)

With many games, the hope of ever winning dies with the player's middle years, when the legs give out. The fascination of Golf, however, is that the player is able to carry his frustration into old age. It is not uncommon to see men well into their nineties tottering about the links, still bent on beating the game that is indomitable.

To a Golfer, three score and ten is par for the course.

One reason for this is the method of scoring in Golf. Golf is one of the few games in which the objective is to have as low a score as possible. Gin rummy is another such game. Both rummy and Golf are card games. In Golf the player takes only one card to start the game. He later discards it, by tearing it into very small pieces and tossing the confetti over his head. He may also say "Gin!" but the male Golfer is more likely to order a double Scotch.

At the outset the Golfer looks upon his scorecard as a document of virgin promise. No matter how many times his scorecard proves to be an update of the Egyptian Book of the Dead, he is buoyant. Hope springs eternal, when fitted with the proper cleats.

On his card, beside each hole, is printed the length of the hole in yards or metres and a number called *par*. What is par? For most Golfers, it is an idea in the mind of God. For a select few, par is attainable on each of the eighteen holes, provided that the Golfer has led a life of virtue and chosen the right broker. The elect may know the yet greater bliss of a *birdie* (one under par), an *eagle* (two under par), or a *hole-in-one* (the divine essence). The number of strokes the Golfer needed, holing out in par or under, he inscribes on his card as a clear, eminently legible figure. This contrasts with his recording a *bogey* (one over par), a *double bogey* (two over par), a *triple bogey*, or symptoms of digital amnesia, which is the total breakdown of that part of the brain that computes arithmetic sums. When the Golfer's strokes for the hole number in this range, his

scorecard testifies to the weakness of Arabic numerals. His 7 is readily taken for a 2, the 8 for a 3, and the 11 for an ace that hiccuped.

At the conclusion of the round, the Golfer adds up the strokes for the eighteen holes and signs the card. If the total is under 100 he signs his own name. If over 100, he signs as "A.N. Other." His signature may also differ considerably from that recognized by his bank, his mother, and the handwriting expert who has had no experience with sand traps.

The Golfer's rare moments of religious ecstasy are closely linked to counting by tens. That is, he first aspires to break 100, then 90, then 80, and finally to break 70. To break 60 is the decimal equivalent of the Second Coming. So long as he has a round number to break, life has meaning for the Golfer.

Because all men are created equal except for the purposes of laying a side bet, the Golfer often has a *handicap*. Golf, as a game for the handicapped, encourages the Golfer to work hard to reduce the manual problem of taking a twenty-dollar bill from his wallet and handing it to his opponent. The Golfer's handicap is like the Renaissance codpiece: it represents an artificial advantage. For this reason some Golfers are shy about revealing it. When a Golfer tells you his handicap, you may be sure that you have won his trust. Which will be the only thing you win from him all day.

The two methods of losing a bet in Golf are (1) *match play*, played for matches, the stakes going to the Golfer winning the greatest number of holes, and (2) *medal play*, in which a medal is awarded (often posthumously) to the Golfer whose card says he took the fewest strokes for the round.

The Golf wager lends extra importance to *the sins of Golf*. Cracking one's joints, for example, as one's opponent is about to strike the ball is a cardinal sin when there is money on the line. As is having gastric juices that gurgle "No way." Club members whose bodies are incapable of complete silence during a money game are inevitably excommunicated, in that no one buys them a drink. These Golfers usually end up, rather pitifully, in the Hades of an amusement-park miniature Golf course, where the background noise level is high enough to drown out all but the loudest of anatomical detonations.

One of the lesser sins of Golf is failing to invite a following group of Golfers to play through. This is a sin of pride. No Golfer cares to admit that his progress to the green is so tortured that he is holding up the foursome behind. He will fail to notice that the players

Play out of bounds

to his rear are stalled by his faltering play, no matter how creatively they dramatize their being impeded: setting up tents, lighting camp fires, and sending ahead messengers to inquire if his party has been stricken by an outbreak of sleeping sickness.

The righteous thing to do in this circumstance is for the Golfer to wave the waiting ones through with the generous, open-handed gesture with which royalty greets the multitude. He should definitely not use an upward thrust of the middle finger, wiggled as a concession to advancement.

Another mild profanation is to tee up one's ball on the fairway. Winter rules permit this, but for some Golfers winter is the longest season of the year, running from July 1 to June 30. Although the Golfer dons mittens to tee up his ball on the fairway, and makes a perform-ance of shivering and slapping his arms around his body to keep warm, though the temperature is 25°C, his conduct is unbecoming. If the course is situated south of the sixtieth parallel, the Golfer may be told to turn in his mukluks.

Playing out of turn. Order of play is not determined by the player who can run fastest to his ball and hit it. This is gauche. The player whose ball is farthest from the hole is said to be *away*, or first to play. If his ball is really distant from the hole he may be away for some time, having left the country. Or he may strike at the ball, causing it to hop a few feet, and find that he is still away. His ball may hit a tree, bouncing back and making the Golfer farther away than he was to start with. Meanwhile, the other players in his group are waiting for him to stop being away, so that they may resume normal living. This can be a difficult time in a Golfer's life, being away for long periods without even the comfort of a letter from home.

The Golfer who drives a long ball, on the other hand, is rarely away on the fairway. He is accustomed to waiting graciously to be the last to take his second shot. It is not considered seemly for him to read a book, pick his nose, or otherwise suggest a lack of interest in the fortunes of those whose balls have put them away. He may also be in an exposed position, and find his yawn reinforced by an errant sphere. In Golf, waiting for one's turn is a special discipline in itself. Its golden rule: wait unto others as you would have them wait unto you.

On the green, the player who is away may have his ball *stymied* by the ball of another lying in the path of his putt. It used to be that the owner of the nearer ball could leave it there, in hopes that his opponent's putt would hit it and move it closer to the cup. This was crude, ungentlemanly conduct, excusable only if the player was raised in a family of lawn bowlers. The correct procedure now is for the Golfer to pick up his ball, regardless of whether another ball is likely to hit it, and replace it with a marker, such as a dime, a tiddly wink, or a partially consumed breath mint. The marker must be placed behind the ball before the ball is lifted. Picking the ball up first, then placing the marker closer to the hole, is clumsy, especially when combined with stepping on the opponent's ball.

Before leaving the subject of soul-trying obstacles, we need to say something about *women's Golf*. Male Golfers, particularly those on in years, have been known to mutter that women should not be allowed to become Golfers. Their objection is for the same reason as that against women becoming priests, namely that they are unable to explore the full depths of misery.

Some male Golfers go so far as to interpret a female on the course as a loose impediment. While it is true that a woman Golfer is a natural object (unless she is wearing a padded bra or other obstruction), she may not be removed. Picking up a woman Golfer is permitted only in the mixed clubhouse lounge. On the course, the male Golfer who finds that his ball lies blocked by a woman Golfer must (a) wait till she moves out of the way in the fullness of time; or (b) invite her to lie down in the grass with him and discuss approaches.

Yet another objection to women Golfers is that their presence inhibits communication between the male player and his ball, when it takes a fancy to a ravine. With a ladies' foursome waiting at the tee, the old-fashioned Golfer (sometimes called "a gentleman") feels constrained to stifle expression of his exasperation, thereby rupturing his spleen. This repression is doubly damaging when the senior Golfer then hears a young female Golfer utter an obscenity that would startle a swamper on a garbage truck.

A less substantial charge laid against women is that some of them take up Golf mainly because the electric Golf car is one vehicle that a woman can park without having to get close to the curb. Statistics show, however, that a woman is the safer driver of the Golf car, even though she drives it around the course backwards. She is less affected by her last shot than is a man, and is therefore less likely to lay rubber on a groundskeeper.

The most crushing blow to prejudice against the women Golfers has been their emergence as *professionals*. In the past men have regarded the female Golf pro as a freak of nature, living on endorsement of corn plasters. But the pro tours for women, and the Sunday

The spectator sport

devotions of TV to these events, have convinced all but the most bigoted male that the woman Golfer can turn professional without growing a moustache. Male Golfers no longer avoid the ladies' tee in fear of developing enlarged breasts. They know that if she knows how to move her hips a woman can make good money as a pro—even on the Golf course.

In appearance—stature, dress, number of limbs—the Golf professional looks like a common mortal. We cannot understand his unique place in the pantheon of sport till we see that he is *the professional's professional*. Pros in other sports look forward to the end of their season so that they can play Golf. Rarely does one hear of a Golf pro who is impatient for the tour to be over so that he can get out and play ice hockey or football. The Golf pro is thus the most blessed of saints. The faithful flock about him, wherever he appears in the tournament, to gaze in awed silence at his eminence. They are genuinely shocked when his ball goes into the lake, and he doesn't walk on the water to reach it. Whence comes this idolatry?

First, the Golf pro is a martyr to the supreme ordeal. He has survived the cut. The cut, administered by an excessive number of strokes on the first or second round of a tournament, is the most excruciating pain the pro can have inflicted on him, as it amputates him from the prize money.

Secondly, the Golf pro can become a living legend. Again like Ulysses, he has made his way past so many monsters—including the Cyclops that is the TV camera—that he is deemed to have supernatural powers. Ordinary Golfers follow Arnold Palmer about, during a tournament, in hopes of absorbing some of the magic that carried the master safely between the Scylla of sand traps and the Charybdis of creek.

Finally, when his powers begin to wane, the fabled Golfer continues to serve his divine mission by travelling the land to consecrate new Golf courses. His crosier has a power grip. His benign air lures a lot of learners onto the course who might otherwise have preserved their sanity.

The holy father of Golf also allows his name to be used to endow many otherwise mundane commercial properties with the glow of transcendent glory. Golfers choose E. F. Hutton as their broker because Tom Watson anointed the investment firm to tee up his nest egg. They buy the Jack Nicklaus Calendar, in hopes of playing out the year in under 365. Such are the powers ordained by Golf.

Is Golf for Eternity?
The Agony and The
Ecstasy

Zealot

*he hole is greater
than the sum of the putts."*

(Golf joke in questionable taste)

From the evidence of the preceding chapters we may conclude that God created Golf in order to make it easier for man to accept his mortality. The Psalms abound in reference to Golf as a spiritual reward: "He maketh me to lie down in green pastures", "My cup runneth over", "He putteth down one and setteth up another."

What remains to be decided is: Can Golf become a universal religion, or is it necessarily restricted to people who drink?

On the plus side, we note that the magnificent obsession that is Golf can seize persons regardless of their physical size. Here it has a broader evangelism than, say, basketball. In Golf great height provides no advantage, except that the very tall Golfer can eat the lower branches of trees blocking his shot. This edge is offset by the altitude of his head making it difficult for him to distinguish his ball from similar objects, such as certain varieties of round, white mushroom. (The penalty for hitting a mushroom instead of one's ball is one stroke and possible arrest for distributing a hallucinogen.)

But it is the spiritual quality of Golf, the inner game, that sets Golf apart from mere sport. Golf is for the person who seeks to make his peace with the Maker (Titleist). How, then, does Golf affect the lifestyle of the believer? To attain the degree of inner peace required, how many Golfers maintain the diet of the ascetic (bamboo shoots, petrified apricots, seaweed, etc.)? Do a significant number of Golfers abstain from sex before playing a round? Professional Frank Beard says "I have known players over the years who have refused to have sex the night before they competed." Since most tournaments begin on Thursday, this means that millions of acolyte Golfers develop a headache on Wednesday night. This puts considerable strain on the sexual relationship, unless

Religious transport

the partner is prepared to think of Monday and Tuesday as a dirty weekend. Being a Golf widow is trying enough, but even more to be pitied is the Golf virgin, she or he who has been incautious enough to agree to the spouse's taking along the clubs on the honeymoon.

At what point does Golf cease to be a cult and become a major religion? Answer: when more people can afford the distillation of the spirit. Like other ministerial programs, televised Golf is observed on Sundays, but at a better time—the afternoon. Says *Golf Digest* of the TV mission: "While the viewing audience for golf may not be as large as that for, say, baseball, it is an audience of wealthier, higher-educated consumers. It is an upscale audience tailored to the advertising messages of auto makers, investment firms, insurance companies and the like." The Compleat Golfer drives a Monte Carlo, is insured against everything but his being carried off the course by a large bird, and wouldn't be found dead holding a bottle of domestic beer.

Roman Catholicism is the church of the poor, Golf the faith of the rich. That it is easier for a camel to go through the eye of a ncdlc than for a rich man to enter into the kingdom of God, does not faze the Golfer so long as he can squeeze past the membership committee.

It follows that the world-wide ministry of Golf depends a great deal on the state of each nation's economy. Conversion is slow in lands such as East Africa, Malaysia, and the Canadian Maritimes. While some disciples may be prepared to endure spikes screwed into their bare feet, Golf will not rival Hinduism or Buddhism till its agony is universally affordable.

Meanwhile, for the wealthy of the western world, Golf takes the traditional hair shirt, adds patch pockets and makes it reversible.

If John Bunyan had played Golf, instead of enjoying the relative serenity of a jail cell, *Pilgrim's Progress* would have been over eighteen holes. Doubting Castle, property of Giant Despair, survives in the flag and the treacherous moat. The Delectable Mountains, the Slough of Despond, the Valley of the Shadow of Death—the allegory is but a crude and primitive predecessor of playing the Golf course with one's son-in-law.

Dangerous Cults: Technocracy

Each hole of Golf is a microcosm of the life experience. The ovum is placed on the tee. It is subjected to a force largely controlled by the involuntary muscles. Projected into the world, the egg flies forth, possibly to land in lush grass, perhaps never to be seen again. After many adventures, the nomad, the symbol of finite existence, is popped into a hole in the ground. The Golfer says a few words. The words are rarely printable, but they do express a sense of loss.

The main difference between Golf and crossing over to the next life is that in Golf the bridge is slippery when wet.

Thus we see that Golf has a divine mission, in making humble even the mightiest of men. This messianic role is typified by the story that is part of the catechism of every devout Golfer:

One day Jesus and Moses returned to Earth for a round of golf. Faced with a long approach shot over a lake, Jesus chose a nine iron.

"Are you crazy?" exclaimed Moses. "You'll never make it with a nine."

"Nonsense. Jack Nicklaus uses a nine," said Jesus, and he promptly pooped his ball into the lake. "Do me a favour, Moses," he said, "do your stuff parting the waters so I can get my ball out."

"No way," Moses responded. "I told you you wouldn't make it, but you insisted on trying it. You do your stuff—walk on over and get it out. After all, you got it in there."

"No," Jesus demurred. "I'll just try another ball."

"Still with a nine iron? You really are crazy, you know you can't make it," Moses said.

"If Nicklaus can, so can I," Jesus retorted, as he hit a beautiful chip directly into the lake.

This happened three more times. "Well I can't afford to keep using new ones," Jesus muttered, walking out on the waters to collect his balls.

Just then another twosome approached, stopping in wonderment as they saw Jesus out on the lake. "Who the hell does he think he is—Jesus Christ?" exclaimed one of them.

"No," retorted Moses. "Jack Nicklaus."

Golf: why the self-made man is recalled by the manufacturer. Because there, but for the grace of Golf, goes God.

Sacro-mental Quiz: "Are You a Golf Fanatic?"

1. Do you picture the Elysian Fields as 36 holes without a bunker?
2. Would you sell your soul to the Devil for:
   (a) the most beautiful woman/man in the world?
   (b) all the gold in the world?
   (c) a birdie on the 18th?
3. In adding up your scorecard, do you regularly subtract ten for neatness?
4. Did you find the inspiration to play Golf because you heard Voices from on high? How did you get high?
5. Many Golfers think of their own home as the 20th hole. Try to describe it without using your hands.
6. How many angels can dance on the head of a pin? Why do they all leave when you take the pin out?
7. The pro shop asks you to make up a twosome with a 60-lb. midget. The midget steps up to the tee and drives his ball 250 yards straight down the middle. Do you:
   (a) tee up your ball?
   (b) tee up the midget?
   (c) fake a heart attack, taking care to use the midget to break your fall?

8. Can you read a green without moving your lips?
9. If you miss your Sunday round of Golf, do you go to confession? Who listens?
10. You probably bought this book in hopes that it would improve your Golf. Has this been a lesson to you?

Photograph By Christopher Nicol

Photograph by Blair Pinder

Eric Nicol started his Golf career as a caddy, during the Depression. Because he was a skinny kid and had a big nose, he was popular with Golfers who were too poor to buy a set of clubs. He still associates Golf with his being shoved into a bag and tossed into the trunk of a car.

Asked which is his favorite course, Nicol always says "Dessert."

Dave More was born in Scotland, but that hasn't helped his golf at all. Environmental protection groups suggest More would be kinder to the landscape if he painted it, rather than hacked it to shreds. Several painting groups have suggested he take up golf.

Golf clubs courtesy Howard Price
Shirt courtesy Evan Penny
Hat by accident